High School Musicals™

# MUSIC and SINGING

rosen publishing's
rosen
central®

New York

Doretta Lau

*In memory of George Lau*

Published in 2010 by The Rosen Publishing Group, Inc.
29 East 21st Street, New York, NY 10010

**Library of Congress Cataloging-in-Publication Data**

Lau, Doretta.
Music and singing / Doretta Lau.—1st ed.
        p. cm.—(High school musicals)
Includes bibliographical references and index.
ISBN-13: 978-1-4358-5262-4 (library binding)
ISBN-13: 978-1-4358-5538-0 (pbk)
ISBN-13: 978-1-4358-5539-7 (6 pack)
1. Musicals—Production and direction. I. Title.
MT955.L3765 2010
782.1'4—dc22

                                                  2008051805

*Manufactured in Malaysia*

# Contents

# INTRODUCTION

The most memorable elements of a musical theater production are often music and singing. Songs like "Memory" from *Cats*, "Do Re Mi" from *The Sound of Music*, "Music of the Night" from *The Phantom of the Opera*, and "I Got Rhythm" from *Girl Crazy* (and later, the film *An American in Paris*) allow a singer to explore a character and make the audience remember the production long after the final curtain.

A good musical production has inspiring songs and well-trained singers. For a high school musical, a carefully chosen production and well-cast singers can be the difference between a hit and a flop. Everyone in a high school musical has to work hard, practice diligently, and collaborate with other students and teachers in order to stage a fantastic show.

Performers Letitia Dean and Norman Bowman work with singers in the company, as well as backstage crew, to stage *High School Musical* for audiences at London's Apollo Theatre Hammersmith.

In addition to singers, there are many musical theater positions related to music and singing. There is a big backstage team that works together to make the singers shine onstage. The musical director, assistant musical director, sound designer, conductor, and the musicians in the orchestra or band all contribute to the musical numbers.

Many musical theater stars began their careers while still in high school. Dame Julie Andrews began singing early on. Her mother, Barbara, and stepfather, Ted, were both performers. They were a vaudeville duo who toured around England performing musical numbers. Ted wanted to have a close relationship with his stepdaughter, so he gave her voice lessons. It was then that Barbara and Ted discovered their daughter possessed a powerful four-octave-range voice.

By high school, Julie Andrews was performing in pantomimes, which are British holiday performances for children. Her career continued to soar. In 1953, she received her first big break: director Vida Hope asked her to star in the Broadway staging of the London hit musical *The Boy Friend*. Andrews almost declined because she didn't want to leave England and her family, but her family convinced her to take the job. Opening night of *The Boy Friend* fell on Andrews's nineteenth birthday. Critics adored her performance. She became a teen sensation, a bona fide Broadway star.

As you can see, the magic of musical theater can begin with performances during high school. A high school musical is the time for singers, conductors, musicians, and sound technicians to experiment like Julie Andrews did with vaudeville. From preproduction planning to auditions to rehearsals, there are many opportunities for students to learn theater craft and gain valuable onstage and backstage experience.

# Preparing to Mount a Musical

The music in a musical begins with the composer. A composer writes the music, from the high notes for a soprano's solo to the low notes of a bassoon's accompaniment. He or she creates a starting point for the director, musical director, and singer to work with and interpret. Without the work of a composer, it would be impossible to stage a musical production. There would be no music!

## Key Backstage Roles for Music and Singing

The director handles the coordination of all the elements that happen onstage and backstage. A musical director, known as an MD, supports the director and is in charge of all the music and singing in the production. The MD may be a student, the music or choir teacher, or a parent with musical theater experience. The most important thing is that the musical director possesses previous

The musical director is responsible for all the music and singing in a musical theater production. He or she begins preparing for the production even before the first actor or actress is cast.

musical training and has an understanding of all the responsibilities included in the position. The musical director will attend all auditions, rehearsals, and performances. It is his or her job to teach the cast the music during rehearsals, play the piano to accompany the singers (or find someone willing to do the job), and assemble the band or orchestra that will play the accompaniment during

performances. As well, the MD works with the sound designer to execute the technical auditory elements of the production. For the performances, the MD may conduct the band or orchestra, or train a conductor.

If a student at school writes the musical, the director will work with the student composer to realize the musical vision. However, it is more likely that a professional composer and librettist will have written the score and book. In this case, the director and the musical director will work together to achieve the right sound and emotion resonance for the production.

Should there be many volunteers working on the backstage crew, the musical director can appoint an assistant musical director. If the musical director is a music teacher at the school, the assistant musical director should be a student who can learn all about the production process. There may also be a singing captain; perhaps the choral teacher can assist here and guide the musical director when necessary. There may also be a band or orchestra, depending on the number of musicians at your school. If it is impossible to assemble a band or orchestra, the show can be accompanied by a piano. The best thing to do is to team up with the school's music teacher, who can teach the score of the musical in band class, eliminating the need for scheduling additional practices before or after school.

## Choosing a Musical

An important step to take when staging a musical at your school is to do thorough research. This may require watching and listening to many musicals before finding one that is suitable for your high school. In all likelihood, your school will stage a show that has been previously produced. The producer, director, and musical director should work together to compile a list of their favorite musical numbers and shows. The team should consult with students interested in musical theater to help with the process of choosing the right production to mount. This list is a starting point to work from and will help direct the research.

When researching musicals for your school, there are a number of things to keep in mind. How many students do you think will be interested in auditioning for the show? Are there singers at school capable of performing in the range required for the roles in the musical you are considering? There is no use in choosing a show that requires a huge cast if the student body is small, or one with a lead baritone if no one can sing the part. The singers and musicians at your school are among the most important resources for your

Choosing a musical begins with research. This means listening to dozens of musical soundtracks and watching DVDs of previously staged productions. A trip to the library is in order.

musical. You must consider their talents and limitations when choosing a production to stage.

One of the best places to find information on musicals is the library. There, you will be able to borrow books on musical theater history, as well as DVDs and soundtracks of musicals. Take notes on the musicals you liked, noting the size of the cast, the number of female and male parts, and whether the show requires an orchestra or band to play the accompanying music. As well, you may want to note the name of the composer and the stars of the show for each musical you wish to consider. This will give you leads on other productions that you may want to explore. One musical you wish to stage may require too many resources, but another by the same composer may need a smaller cast and less elaborate sets.

The Internet is another good place to conduct research. If you refer to the Web sites section at the back of this book, you will find a number of URLs for musical theater Web pages. Sites like the Cyber Encyclopedia of Musical Theatre, TV, and Film; the Guide to Musical Theatre; Musical Heaven; and Musical Stages contain current information and links to numerous resources, such as reviews, sample lyrics from shows, and the history of musical theater. If you read about a musical that interests you, try finding clips on video streaming sites like YouTube. Watching and listening to performances is the best way to discover whether or not the music and singing in a show is right for your school musical.

Once the research is complete, narrow the list down to three musicals. When making this list, it is wise to find out if the shows you are considering are available for performance. If a professional producer in your area has already acquired the rights to performance, your school will not be able to stage that particular show. Generally, agents will not allow high schools access to musicals that can still draw audiences in professional markets. For instance, *The Rocky Horror Show*, which premiered in 1973, has never been contracted to an amateur production company because it still packs theaters around the world.

Before making a final decision on the show to mount, it's best to have a look at the full script, known as the libretto or the book. In order to gain access to a copy of the libretto, scores, instrumental arrangements, and band parts, you will have to write to a music publishing company to ask for "perusal material." The material may also come with demo tapes. Companies like Music Theater International; Tams-Witmark; Dramatists' Play Service; Musicscope; Samuel French; Broadway Play Publishing, Inc.; Rodgers and Hammerstein Musical Library; and Josef Weinberger control the international performance rights for many musicals and will lend the material for a short period of time. Do not photocopy or scan the perusal material; these actions would violate copyright laws.

The director and musical director should go through the perusal material together, examining the book and the score. The musical director should identify whether or not the school has both the singing and musical talent to carry off the show, as well as a proper venue for all the staging needs. It is important that there are enough students at the school who have the skill to sing and play the music, or the production will fail. The director and musical director should read aloud the entire book to get a sense of how the words sound spoken and to determine if the material is suitable for high school students to perform or watch. If possible, the musical director should ask students to sing the songs to see how the vocal parts sound in a live setting. This is also an opportunity to figure out if the musical focuses too much on a single performer; it is better to stage a show that allows a number of students the opportunity to perform

The director and musical director should meet to go over perusal material for the show that they are interested in staging. It is important to examine the book and score carefully.

solos, rather than a show that makes one student the obvious star. It is too much to ask a single student to carry an entire production on the strength of his or her performance.

When the director and musical director have decided on a musical to stage, it is time to apply for performance rights through an agent. The agent will want to know the dates and location of the performance, ticket price, venue size, and whether you will use an orchestra or solo piano for the accompanying music. There will

## To Do List for Choosing a Musical

- Research musicals carefully, keeping in mind the limits of your resources for staging a show.
- Find out if the show you want is available for performance in your town or city.
- Request perusal material from a music publishing company.
- The director, producer, and musical director should study the perusal material to help decide if the musical is suitable for your school.
- Apply for performance rights.
- Sign the contract with the agent who represents the musical you wish to perform.

either be a set fee per performance or a percentage of gross ticket sales between 7.5 and 12.5 percent.

Once the agent grants your school the right to perform the music, he or she will issue a contract. The contract will cover specific details about your show, including:

- The name of the venue.
- The dates and the number of performances.
- A promise that the school will perform the show as it is printed in the libretto and score, without any changes.
- An outline of the royalties and fees for borrowing the libretto and score, as well as a timeline for when these fees must be paid.
- A request for the author and publishing company credits to appear in publicity materials and the show program.

- A deadline for the return of all performance materials lent by the publishing company.
- Two tickets for each performance must be set aside for the rights owner.
- An exclusion clause stating what rights are not included with performance rights, such as radio and television broadcasting.
- A cancellation clause allowing the rights owners to charge even if a show is cancelled.

Once the contract is signed, the school is legally bound to produce the show under the specific guidelines set by the agent. The agent supplies the school with the score, libretto, and vocal books for a period of three months. All materials will be returned to the agent at the end of the show's run; therefore, markings on the materials should be made in pencil only and erased when the show is done. Instrumental parts are sent later in the rehearsal process and are on loan for about a month. The musical director is in charge of ensuring that none of the material is damaged during rehearsals. Everyone involved should treat the score, libretto, and vocal books with care. The school production may be an amateur one, but the attitude of every student should be professional.

## Preparing for Auditions: Director and Musical Director

Once the school has acquired performance rights to a musical, the director and musical director meet to go through the entire score. The director should make a list of all the characters with names, noting whether they are male or female. Start with the leading roles first, and descend in order of the size or importance of a role.

Identify the vocal range required for each character: soprano, alto, tenor, and baritone/bass. If this information is not clearly written in the score, consult with the musical director to determine the vocal range requirements for each character. Write a general description for each character. This will make it easier to determine the general look the actor should have for the role.

To simplify the casting process, the director should make a grid with each character's name down the left and each scene across

Every part in a musical is written for a specific vocal range: soprano, alto, tenor, and baritone/bass. In general, most women sing soprano or alto.

the top. Mark off the scenes in which each character appears, noting whether he or she has a singing part in that particular scene. Crowd scenes should be identified as "male chorus" and "female chorus," depending on the characters needed for the scene. Using the character grid, the director will be able to determine how many actors are needed for the production. Actors can double on certain small roles if the characters do not appear onstage at the same time during any point in the musical.

When casting the chorus, keep in mind the size of the stage and if it will be hard to schedule a large number of actors for rehearsals and train each individual properly. The director will work with the MD and the choreographer to decide on the right number of chorus members. Though it is admirable to have a grand artistic vision involving a large cast, one must consider the costume budget when making casting decisions. There is no use in having a huge cast if there isn't enough money for proper costumes.

## Main Responsibilities of a Musical Director

The musical director is responsible for all the musical elements in the production. The MD attends auditions, assesses the singing ability of performers, and assists with casting. It is an advantage for an MD to be a pianist so that he or she can play the accompaniment during rehearsals. The MD teaches the cast the music.

The musical director can supervise the band or appoint someone to do so. The MD rehearses with the band before the band works with the cast. As well, he or she works with the sound designer to achieve the right sound balance in the performance space. The MD conducts the show or finds someone to conduct.

Above all, when casting for a musical, an actor's vocal talent is his or her most important trait to assess. Even if an actor looks perfect for a role, if he or she cannot sing, then he or she is not a strong candidate for the part. The sound of the musical can only be as good as the weakest singer.

## How to Run an Audition

Spread the word about the audition for your musical via the school newspaper, social networking programs, blogs, posters, and in-class announcements. Make sure that the drama and music class teachers are aware of the auditions so that they can encourage the students taking their courses to participate in the production. The musical director may want to hold information sessions for actors who have never auditioned for musical theater to help with song choice prior to the auditions.

The director should make a sign-up sheet and schedule for the auditions and post them on a bulletin board. The sign-up sheet should have a space for students to leave their contact information. Students who are interested in auditioning can book their own audition dates and times. When making the schedule, note that singing auditions take ten minutes, and combined singing and acting auditions take fifteen minutes. As well, it is very important to build breaks into the audition schedule because judging singers and actors is a lengthy and tiring process for the director and musical director.

On audition days, a volunteer should greet and organize the singers as they arrive in a waiting area for their appointments. The director and musical director will remain in the audition room for the entire day, except during breaks. Each singer should be shown into the audition room once the director and musical director are ready.

An audition does not have to be nerve wracking. In fact, it can be quite fun! Proper preparation and a positive attitude will make the experience less stressful.

The musical director should not double as the accompanist during auditions; he or she should be able to sit back and assess the merits of each singer without any extra distractions. An excellent pianist, with experience accompanying singers, should be recruited to play for auditions.

When assessing an actor's voice, consider the tone, vocal strength, and style of singing. Does the singer have good diction? Will the audience be able to understand the lyrics of the song? Does the singer have the ability to bring forth the right emotions to match the lyrics in the song?

The director and musical director should be polite to all students who audition, regardless of individual talent and skill. However, it is within reason to stop a singer who has sung for too long. If a singer shows promise after the first song, ask him or her to sing a second song to further assess ability. At the end of the audition, thank and dismiss the singer. When the director and musical director are alone, they should have an immediate discussion about the singer and make notes for the meeting at the end of the day.

When all the auditions are complete, the director, musical director, and choreographer can decide who should receive a callback, which is a second audition. During callbacks, singers may be asked to perform duets to give a sense of what the show will sound like with certain students in the roles. Keep in mind that lead roles should have understudies in case a lead falls sick during the run or drops out of the production partway through. Understudies may have smaller roles in the production or be part of the chorus.

# 2
### CHAPTER

# Audition Tips for Singers

**A**n audition is similar to a job interview: it is a chance to make a good impression and convey one's abilities and personality in a short period of time. The best way to leave a great impression on the director and music director is to understand the audition process and practice the right songs. No amount of talent can replace the need for careful preparation. Even the most accomplished Broadway performer must prepare for an audition.

At an audition, performers sing with piano accompaniment. Therefore, the best way to practice is with a pianist playing the accompanying music. This way, it will not feel strange to sing along with live piano music on the day of the audition. An audition will often make a singer nervous, so it is best to make the process feel as familiar and comfortable as possible. The more familiar a situation is, the less scary it becomes. If a friend or family member knows how to play, ask him or her to help with practice sessions. The music or choir teacher at school is a good person to ask for

When preparing to audition for a musical theater role, ask a friend, family member, or your vocal instructor to be your accompanist when you are practicing your songs.

preparation help if you do not have access to a piano at home or at a friend's house. You may be able to get permission to practice on a school piano.

## Choosing Audition Songs

Depending on the preference of the director and the musical director, you may either be given songs from the musical to sing, or you will have to prepare a few different songs. When singing auditions are announced, make sure that you find out what you need to prepare.

If you aren't given music to perform, you should prepare a minimum of two songs for an audition. Each song should be roughly two minutes in length; you may wish to reduce longer

### Five Tips to Remember for Callbacks

1. Wear the same clothes and hairstyle you wore to the audition.
2. Bring the same two songs you sang at the first audition. Have additional songs prepared.
3. If you are permitted to sing songs other than the two that you first sang, perform your most exciting and electrifying song.
4. If you are unable to sing a song they ask for, it is better to say that you do not have that kind of song prepared than risk a sloppy performance of a song you do not know.
5. Always listen to the director and wait for instructions. Do not ask if you can sing additional songs; you will be invited to sing more if the director wants to hear more from you.

songs to a single verse and chorus. If possible, try to find short numbers to perform so that the song feels complete during the audition. A song in a musical is like a monologue in a play—it is an opportunity to give life to a character. Essentially, singers must act their songs. Therefore, when singing an audition song, you should be in character.

When you perform your audition song, you should be acting the song while you are singing it. In order to do this well, you must understand the character you are playing.

The songs selected should showcase the voice—choosing the right song will highlight strengths and mask possible weaknesses. For contrast, one song should be a ballad and the other should be an up-tempo song. The ballad is an opportunity for a singer to showcase emotional range as well as the ability to phrase lyrics with sensitivity and intelligence. The up-tempo song allows

a performer to entertain and reveal technical abilities like rhythm. Singing an up-tempo song is a chance to show the director and musical director your sparkling personality, so choose a funny song. Above all, a singer should aim to entertain in any situation, whether in an audition or onstage. The last thing you want to do is bore your audience.

In addition to the ballad and the up-tempo song, it is wise to have an additional three to four songs prepared in case the director asks for another song after you have already sung the ballad and up-tempo song. There is nothing worse than being unprepared when a director is interested in your performance. Therefore, singers might also want to prepare a comedy song, a contemporary rock song, and a patter song. Girls can also add a standard torch song to their audition repertoire. If there is time, it is wise to practice an additional song for each category in case other people at the audition sing the same song as you. This means that you may have up to twelve songs at your disposal in any audition.

## Ten Tips to Remember on Audition Day

1. Visit the restroom before the audition.
2. Bring something to do while you wait for your turn. Do not spend the waiting time worrying about how you will perform.
3. Find out how many people you will be auditioning in front of before you enter the audition room.
4. Know what you are going to sing before the audition begins.
5. Walk into the audition room with purpose and focus.
6. Do not place your personal belongings on the piano or the director's table. Put them next to the door when you enter.
7. Avoid excessive chatter with the director and musical director.
8. Do not stand too close to the piano or the people for whom you are auditioning.
9. Do not use props in your performance.
10. Listen to the director and follow his or her instructions. Do not ask questions like, "How many songs should I sing?"

Standing out from the crowd is very important if there are many students auditioning for few parts. Singing a song that is fresh to the director and musical director will help in establishing your individual talent.

Noel Coward, Howard Dietz, Frank Loesser, Cole Porter, E. Y. Harburg, and Lorenz Hart have written good comedy songs that are suitable for auditions. It may be difficult to find a comedy song that suits your range and abilities—you may have to listen to many songs before you find the right one to perform. Classics like "Take Back the Mink," "Well, Did You Evah?" and "Why Do the Wrong People Travel?" are funny and give singers the chance to show off a sense of humor.

The contemporary rock song should have a pretty melody and powerful words. Do not choose a song that has repetitive, nonsensical lyrics. The song should allow the singer to showcase the voice and express emotion. Soft rock songs by such artists as Aerosmith, Michael Jackson, Sheryl Crow, Kid Rock, Kelly Clarkson, and Alicia Keys would be better for an audition. The contemporary song gives students a chance to choose a number that other singers may not perform.

Patter songs have complicated and wordy lyrics. Gilbert and Sullivan, Porter, Coward, and Hart all wrote this type of quick, zingy song. "My Eyes Are Fully Open" from *The Pirates of Penzance* and "Another Hundred People" from *Company* are good examples of patter songs.

For girls, a torch song—a sentimental song, usually about unrequited love—can be a great audition piece. Ethel Merman, Judy Garland, Barbra Streisand, and Ella Fitzgerald have all recorded great interpretations of numerous torch songs. Listen to their records to get a sense of how different singers handle the same songs. What do they do that is similar? What do they do that is unique? How can you apply this information to your own performance? Good audition songs include "First You Have Me High, Then You Have Me Low," "The Man I Love," and "The Man That Got Away."

There are songs that should not be used for auditions. Very well-known songs should be avoided, as should songs that have famous interpretations. If you sing a song like "Over the Rainbow," the listener will likely compare your performance with that of Judy Garland. As well, don't choose difficult songs to perform; it is possible to showcase your voice without selecting a song that might prove hard to sing under stress.

## Dressing for Your Audition

Clothing choice is another important element of the singing audition. Performers should dress neatly and pay attention to grooming. Girls should wear a dress or a skirt with fashionable shoes in a neutral color. Boys should wear a crisp button-down shirt and avoid jeans. (If dance and acting auditions are the same day, be sure to wear something that will accommodate the movements you will need to make for those as well.)

On the day of the audition, you must bring your sheet music with you for every song you intend to sing. Keep your music in a sturdy folder. You may want to fix each page to one side of a piece of cardstock to make it easier for the pianist to handle and play from. It is best to avoid forcing the pianist to make page turns while playing. Do not bring wrinkled, folded, or illegible sheet music to your audition; if the pianist cannot read the music, he or she will not be able to play your song well. The pianist is there to make you sound your best, and he or she should be given the best tools to

Remember that proper clothing and careful grooming will help enhance your audition. A polished appearance tells a director and the casting team that you understand how to act in a professional manner.

help you in your audition. Remember, you want your talents and personality to be the focus of the audition instead of small, careless mistakes that distract from your hard work. Carrying yourself in a professional manner and being prepared will work to highlight your voice and acting skills.

# Rehearsals

The director, choreographer, and musical director draft a rehearsal schedule, keeping in mind both music and dance needs. Ideally, there will be eight weeks of rehearsal time before opening night, with a minimum of four three-hour sessions a week. A weekend rehearsal can be two sessions, with a break in the middle.

## Warming Up

Each music rehearsal should start with a warm-up period. Just like the body, a voice needs to be warmed up before intense use. Singing can be a strain on the voice, so it is important to take good care of it and use proper technique during rehearsals and performances. Feel free to ask the musical director for good warm-up techniques.

During the warm-up, the musical director can run exercises for the vocal cords, diaphragm, lips, and tongue. It is important for singers to focus on posture and breath, gently easing into complex and demanding vocal work. To practice good posture, actors can pretend to be marionettes, with a string attached to the top of their heads. The body should be relaxed and aligned with this

Good posture is key to doing good vocal work. Be sure to stand straight when warming up your voice and to be aware of your posture when you are singing full songs.

imaginary string. After good posture has been established, it is time to do breathing exercises, such as panting like a dog or placing the hands on the diaphragm and breathing deeply to expand it outward.

When posture and breathing exercises are done, it is safe to begin vocal warm-ups. Actors should massage their lips, throats, and faces and rid the body of any lingering tension. Everyone should start humming "mmm" in a gentle fashion, working up and down individual voice ranges. Next, singers should sing scales of round, open vowels, repeating notes as needed. Throughout the warm-up, the breathing should continue to remain deep and relaxed.

## Singing Dos and Don'ts

Throughout the day, singers should drink

plenty of water that is either room temperature or hot in order to keep their vocal cords properly lubricated. Dry vocal cords will lead to a raspy and scratchy voice. It is best to avoid caffeinated drinks like coffee, tea, and sodas because caffeine has a drying effect on the vocal cords. As well, do not eat dairy the day of a rehearsal or performance, as dairy causes mucus to build up in the throat.

Warm-up exercises can be done in a group. During this time, it is important to remember that proper singing comes from deep within the body, not from the throat.

When speaking and singing, do not push the voice from the throat. Singing from the throat over a period of time will damage your voice. The voice should come from deep within the body. You should feel your navel move toward your spine when you are speaking or singing. Remember to take deep breaths and keep the body relaxed and upright.

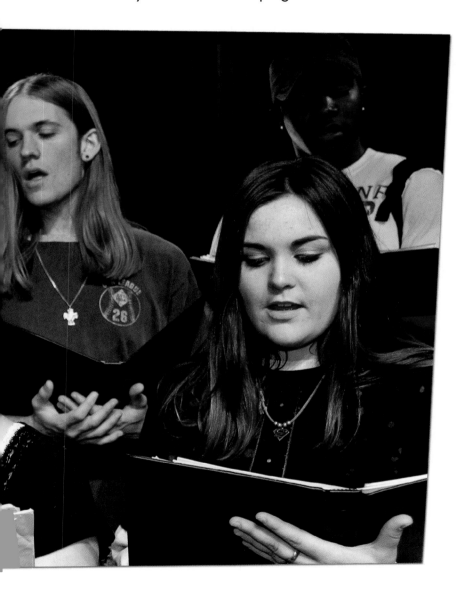

Steam is the best remedy for colds and throat infections. Put hot water into the sink or a large bowl, place a towel over your head, and lean over the steam. Inhale and exhale slowly; be careful not to scald yourself. Each session should be about ten minutes. Repeat several times a day for the best results.

## Learning the Music

The MD will teach the cast the music as soon as

possible. It is best to start with a group song; this will help bring the cast together because starting with something new at the same time encourages teamwork and promotes a sense of camaraderie. For chorus numbers, the musical director will organize cast members by their vocal range. Singers should be gathered near the piano. Each group will work through the songs in sections of eight bars of music. This method of breaking down the song is called note bashing. At the end of the rehearsal, all the vocal groups will gather together and sing what they learned. The most important thing for singers to learn is that a group song is not the time to act as an individual. Chorus members should work together to achieve a well-blended sound.

Each singer will be assigned homework—to practice what he or she learned in rehearsal and to think about the lyrics for the songs

## How to Read a Libretto and Score

A libretto reads differently from a play script. Song lyrics will be printed in verse, like poetry, and may appear in all capital letters. Differing lyrics that should be sung by different characters at the same time will appear side by side. Passages of spoken dialogue accompanied by music, called underscored passages, are marked by a continuous vertical line in the left-hand margin of the libretto. Each song and musical passage will have a number that matches the number in the score and band parts. Some musicals will contain stage and technical directions; these are a guideline only. Stage directions that should be synchronized with the music will be marked in the libretto.

he or she is singing and how the songs help tell a story and further the plot in the musical. The next rehearsal will begin with a review of what was previously taught.

For solos, the same method for learning a song is used. Soloists will learn to work on tempo and delivery to capture and radiate the right emotions for the song. It is important to know that the rests in the song—the silent pauses in the music—are as important to consider as the sung notes themselves. There is a reason why the composer elected to use certain time signatures, tempos, major or minor keys, and volumes for each song. A singer's job is to interpret the music and connect it to the character he or she is playing. The director and musical director will guide each cast member to a good performance, and it is up to each singer to work hard and listen to instructions.

The first big goal of rehearsals is the stagger-through. The stagger-through is the first attempt at running through an entire act or the whole show in sequence without the aid of the libretto and vocal books. Once a stagger-through has been achieved, the musical director can work on the fine details with individual singers.

## Accompanying Music

The director and musical director will decide whether it is appropriate for a band or orchestra to play the music during performances. For a high school production, it is unlikely that there are enough students to make a complete orchestra for a performance. Therefore, it is most likely that a small band will be playing the accompaniment for the show. The band needs about a month of preparation. The musical director rehearses with the band

Members of the school band are the perfect students to recruit to play the accompaniment for a musical. The musical director works with the musicians to prepare for the performance.

in separate music rehearsals, working with musicians to learn and interpret the entire score. The cast and the band do not play together until the final week before the show. The final week is an important time for the vocalists and the musicians to adapt what they have learned to the style of the entire show.

# 4

CHAPTER

# Sound Design and Showtime!

**S**ound design has become a significant aspect in modern musical theater because of new technologies in recording, microcircuitry, sound modification, and digital audio technology. These technologies allow directors to experiment with staging and choreography, accomplishing onstage feats that were not possible before. In response, composers and librettists write musicals that take these technologies and staging developments to new limits, creating more daring and complex productions.

Good sound design is crucial to any musical theater production. A sound designer can enhance the talents of the cast by setting up the right combination of microphones, adjusting sound levels at a mixing board, and placing musicians in the right place in a venue. Live sound is different from recorded sound; there are many variables that can make or break the sound of a performance. On a recording, it is possible to ensure that every word and instrument is clear and at the right audio balance. During a live performance, however, the music and singing will sound different in every part of the theater. It is a sound designer's job to ensure that the music and singing sound good in every seat in the house. While it might seem like a very simple task, it can actually be very challenging.

The sound designer is an important member of the production crew. He or she ensures that every person in the audience can hear every word a singer sings and every note a musician plays.

Recruiting a good sound designer is a step in achieving great sound design. Does your school have a radio station? Or is there an audiovisual club? Members of these two groups will be strong candidates for this job, which requires an understanding of sound, preparing for a production, and technical skills.

The sound designer should read the libretto, making a list of scenes and songs, and noting what sound effects will be needed. Then, he or she should listen to the soundtrack for the show to understand the style of the musical and get a general feel for the show. The soundtrack and the production will not sound exactly the same— the singers will be different, as well as the band or orchestra. After doing this initial preparation, the sound designer should meet with the director and other department heads to find out more about the production. Details like cast size, audience size, venue size, and set decor must be communicated to the sound designer because all of those things affect the way the actors and the music will sound to the audience. The right modifications can really make the show.

The theater space will affect the sound quality of singing and music. No two venues have the same effect on sound. A good sound designer will take every detail and quirk of a venue into consideration when preparing for the production.

## The Performance Space

The sound designer should bring a CD soundtrack of the show and take a cast member to visit the theater space as soon as possible to get a sense of the acoustics. While the cast member sings onstage, the sound designer should listen from different parts of the theater

and take notes on how sound differs from spot to spot. The sound designer should stand onstage and speak to get a sense of what the sound will be like for the actor and to determine how the voice carries in the space.

If the theater has sound equipment, the sound designer should find out what type of PA system there is, how many loudspeakers there are, the location of loudspeakers in the space, and if there are other available output channels. Ask permission to play a CD over the sound system to get a sense of how recorded tracks sound through the loudspeakers. Again, walk around the theater to assess sound quality throughout the venue.

Have a look at where the musicians will be situated. If there isn't an orchestra pit, where might be the best place for them? Perhaps they will be at the back of the stage, in the wings, or near the audience. Placement of the musicians is crucial to sound design for a show.

The venue may not be a theater space. Perhaps the musical will be mounted in the school gymnasium, which will not have the best acoustics. In this case, there will be a need to purchase or rent the following equipment: PA system, microphones, amplifiers, mixing desk, loudspeakers, mini-disc players, and music stands. This can become quite taxing on the budget, so it's best to brainstorm ways to avoid having to spend too much on equipment. Find out what the school already owns, and ask students if they can lend personal equipment to the production or if their siblings or parents might have this equipment. Also, find out if the local sound shops are willing to sponsor the show by lending equipment free of charge or at a lower rate in exchange for mentions in publicity materials and the show program.

When all the equipment has been secured, make a plan for transport. Perhaps a student or teacher has access to a large van. Remember to budget for fuel costs, and be certain there are volunteers strong enough to lift and move heavy sound equipment.

## Microphones for Performers, Musicians, and the Stage

In small theatres, do not use microphones for performances that use few instruments. But in a larger theater, with a large band or full

To ensure that each actor's voice is properly amplified, the sound designer selects the proper microphone and places it on the actor or somewhere on or around the stage.

orchestra, it will likely be necessary to use microphones to boost the singers' sound levels and protect their voices from strain.

To amplify sound onstage, use float microphones near the front of the stage. Rifle microphones can be used to target specific areas like a staircase, balcony, or ceiling. If there is a big enough budget, individual performers can use radio microphones as well.

A good production team makes a performance seem effortless. The backstage crew's attention to detail makes everything that happens onstage appear smooth and seamless.

Radio microphones are powered by batteries the size of a deck of cards and are very small. They can be clipped into the front of a costume or hidden in the hair. It is possible for actors to share radio mics; use the character grid to determine which characters do not share the stage at the same time and rotate the microphones between cast members. Musicians may need to wear microphones as well. The MD and sound designer will work together to figure out which instruments in the band may need a sound level boost to be heard in the theater.

## Sound Effects

The sound designer is responsible for acquiring sound effects and ambient background noise for the production. Every slamming door, thunderstorm, and ringing telephone must be properly represented with the right sound, or the audience will have trouble suspending disbelief for the duration of the show.

After making the initial list of necessary sound effects, the sound designer should consult with the deputy stage manager to see if there are any additional sound effects not apparent in the libretto that have been added to the staging. All effects must be ready for technical and dress rehearsals, so the sound designer must start sourcing effects and planning live sound as soon as possible.

Some of the effects can be prerecorded, while others can be coordinated to occur in the wings during the performance. For ambient background noise, consult with the musical director for what is needed. There may be a need for recordings of traffic, weather, and bird song. However, musicians can play some of these sounds on their instruments during the performance: saxophones can represent sirens, tympanis thunder, and flutes birds singing.

There are a number of resources for prerecorded sound effects. Check with the music and drama teachers to see if there are sound effect recordings from previous productions. For additional effects, search the Internet, local library, and music stores. It may be cheaper for the sound designer to record some of the sound effects that are needed. If this is the case, record several versions of the same sound and let the director choose what will be used in the production. For ambient noise, record twice as much as is needed for a scene; this way, if an actor misses a cue, the ambient noise will not run out before the scene is complete.

When the sound designer has collected all of the final sound effects, he or she must make a master recording of the effects in the order that they must be played. The master recording can be burned onto a CD or organized on a mini disc; check to see what kind of equipment will be available for the dress rehearsal and performances, and choose the format accordingly. When the

## Types of Microphones

- Moving coil or dynamic microphones are used during live performances because they are excellent at capturing the frequency of the human voice.
- Condenser and capacitor microphones use a phantom power supply. Many rifle, float, and radio microphones use this technology.
- Ribbon microphones are very sensitive to sound and are used only in recording studios.
- Omnidirectional microphones can pick up sounds from all directions.
- Cardioid or unidirectional microphones pick up sounds from one direction.
- Hyper-cardioid microphones mainly pick up sounds from one direction but also pick up a limited amount of sound from the opposite direction.
- Bidirectional or figure-of-eight mikes are sensitive to sounds from two directions that are opposite each other.

master recording is complete, make a sound cues sheet for easy reference. The sheet should be organized according to acts, with each cue numbered and showing the corresponding page in the libretto. The kind of sound effect should also be listed, along with the duration the effect will last.

## The Mixing Desk

All microphones and other sound equipment, such as electric instruments and mini-disc players, should be plugged into the input channels of the mixing desk. During performances, the sound designer or an assistant will use the mixing desk to equalize the signals from each input channel, creating a rich and clear sound. The sound is output through amplifiers and loudspeakers around the theater, and should always appear to be coming from the stage.

## Final Rehearsals and Performances

The week of final rehearsals and the opening of the show will run smoothly if everything has been practiced and planned correctly. Everyone involved will follow the production schedule set by the production manager.

The sitzprobe is the last rehearsal before the technical rehearsals begin. This is the first time the cast will sing through the entire show with the band or orchestra, instead of with the piano. The musical director will give final directions to singers during this time. If there are microphones in the production, the next order of business is the sound balance rehearsal, which will involve the musical director, the cast, the band, and the sound designer. This is a chance to work through issues on the mixing board and test the levels needed for each singer and musician.

The technical rehearsals bring together all departments for the first time. Lights, sound, and stage crews will run through the entire show with the cast and band. All technical issues must be sorted out before the two dress rehearsals. Singers should have a call time of an hour before any dress rehearsal or show to ensure that there is time for proper warm-ups. The first dress rehearsal can be done with just piano accompaniment, while the second dress rehearsal should be done with the full band or orchestra.

Finally, it's showtime! Remind everyone in the cast, band, and crew to stay relaxed and calm throughout the performance. After all the practice and organization, things will fall into place. The

Opening night is when all the hard work of the cast and crew comes together in front of an audience for the first time. It's an opportunity for everyone's talents to shine brightly!

director may choose to record the show on opening night so that the musical director can go over the recording to determine if everything went according to plan and to make any needed changes for the rest of the run. Above all, when it's time to perform, everyone involved should remember to have fun and entertain the audience.

**alto** The second-highest voice part in a four-part chorus.

**audition** A trial performance used to evaluate a singer's talents and skill.

**band** A group of musicians that play together as an ensemble.

**band parts** The music for each instrumentalist.

**book** The script of a musical.

**callback** A second or additional audition for a part in a theater production.

**cast** The set of characters for a musical production.

**composer** A person who writes music.

**diction** Clear pronunciation of consonants.

**director** The person in overall control of all artistic and creative elements of a show.

**duet** A musical composition written for two singers.

**float microphone** A microphone that is fixed at the edge of the stage.

**house** The auditorium in which a musical is performed; also the audience.

**lead** A principal actor, usually the largest or most important part in the show.

**librettist** The person who writes the libretto for a musical or opera.

**libretto** The printed script of all dialogue and lyrics.

**MD** Musical director.

**note bash** The initial teaching and learning of vocal lines.

**rest** A rhythmic silence.

**run** Every performance from opening to closing night: "a five-week run"; also a rehearsal without any interruptions.

**sitzprobe**  Rehearsal at which cast members sing with the orchestra but do not act or dance.

**soprano**  The highest voice part in a four-part chorus.

**tenor**  The next-to-lowest voice part in a four-part chorus.

**underscoring**  Music played under dialogue scenes.

**understudy**  An actor who studies another actor's part so that he or she can substitute in case of an emergency.

**vaudeville**  Stage entertainment consisting of various acts, including singers, comedians, and performing animals.

**venue**  The theater or auditorium where the musical will be performed.

## Broadway at the Center

Virginia Musical Theatre, Inc.
228 N. Lynnhaven Road, Suite 114
Virginia Beach, VA 23452
(757) 340-5446
E-mail: office@vmtheatre.org
Web site: http://www.broadwayatthecenter.com
Broadway at the Center is a leading musical theater company.

## The Grand Theatre

471 Richmond Street
London, ON N6A 3E4
Canada
(800) 265-1593
Web site: http://www.grandtheatre.com
This theater has a program called the High School Project, which allows
high school students to learn musical theater craft.

## New Jersey School of Dramatic Arts

593 Bloomfield Avenue
Bloomfield, NJ 07003-2502
(973) 566-9700
E-mail: info@njactors.org
Web site: http://www.njactors.org/summercamp.htm
This is New Jersey's premier acting school, and it runs summer musical
theater camps for teens.

## NYU Steinhardt Summer Program
35 West 4th Street, Suite 777
New York, NY 10012
(212) 998-5424
Web site: http://steinhardt.nyu.edu/music/summer
New York University's Steinhardt Department of Music and Performing
    Arts Professions has a summer program for high school students.

## Theatre Ontario
215 Spadina Avenue, Suite 210
Toronto, ON M5T 2C7
Canada
E-mail: info@theatreontario.org
(416) 408-4556
Web site: http://theatreontario.org
Theatre Ontario is a not-for-profit association of community, educational,
    and professional theater organizations and individuals dedicated to
    high-quality theater.

## Theatre Under the Stars
2099 Beach Avenue
Stanley Park
Vancouver, BC V6G 1Z4
Canada
E-mail: info@tuts.ca
(604) 734-1917
Web site: http://www.tuts.ca
This Canadian musical theater company stages productions for the
    summer months.

**UCLA Arts Camp**
UCLA School of Theater, Film and Television
102 East Melnitz Hall, Box 951622
Los Angeles, CA 90095-1622
(888) 497-3553
E-mail: info@usperformingarts.com
Web site: http://legacy.tft.ucla.edu/artscamp
The UCLA Arts Camp is a summer musical theater conservatory for
students ages sixteen to twenty-two.

**University of Michigan School of Music,
      Theatre & Dance**
E. V. Moore Building
1100 Baits Drive
Ann Arbor, MI 48109-2085
(734) 763-1279
E-mail: michyouthensembles@umich.edu
Web site: http://www.music.umich.edu/special_programs/youth
The University of Michigan has youth summer programs in musical
theater.

## Web Sites

Due to the changing nature of Internet links, Rosen Publishing has
developed an online list of Web sites related to the subject of this
book. This site is updated regularly. Please use this link to access
the list:

http://www.rosenlinks.com/hsm/musi

# FOR FURTHER READING

Boytim, Joan Frey. *The First Book of Broadway Solos: Mezzo-Soprano*. Milwaukee, WI: Hal Leonard Corporation, 2001.

Dansicker, Michael. *Kids' Musical Theatre Audition: Boys' Edition*. Milwaukee, WI: Hal Leonard Corporation, 2007.

Dansicker, Michael. *Kids' Musical Theatre Audition: Girls' Edition*. Milwaukee, WI: Hal Leonard Corporation, 2007.

Friedman, Lisa. *Break a Leg! The Kids' Guide to Acting and Stagecraft*. New York, NY: Workman Publishing Company, 2002.

Kenrick, John. *Musical Theatre: A History*. Harrisburg, PA: Continuum International Publishing Group, 2008.

Lerch, Louise. *The Teen's Musical Theatre Collection: Young Woman's Collection*. Milwaukee, WI: Hal Leonard Corporation, 2001.

Miller, Scott. *Strike Up the Band: A New History of Musical Theatre*. Portsmouth, NH: Heinemann Drama, 2006.

Peterson, Lenka. *Kids Take the Stage: Helping Young People Discover the Creative Outlet of Theater*. New York, NY: Back Stage Books, 2006.

Silver, Fred. *Auditioning for the Musical Theatre*. New York, NY: Penguin, 1988.

Eakle, Kit. "Some Basic Tips for Vocal Health." Retrieved October 19, 2008 (http://www.musickit.com/resources/vocal.html).

Gardyne, John. *Producing Musicals: A Practical Guide.* Ramsbury, England: The Crowood Press Ltd., 2004.

Internet Movie Database. "Julie Andrews." Retrieved October 19, 2008 (http://www.imdb.com/name/nm0000267).

Melton, Joan. *Singing in Musical Theatre: The Training of Singers and Actors.* New York, NY: Allworth Press, 2007.

Novak, Elaine A., and Deborah Novak. *Staging Musical Theatre: A Complete Guide for Directors, Choreographers and Producers.* Cincinnati, OH: Betterway Books, 1996.

Oliver, Donald. *How to Audition for the Musical Theatre: A Step-by-Step Guide to Effective Preparation.* New York, NY: Drama Book Publishers, 1988.

Ratliff, Gerald Lee, and Suzanne Trauth. *On Stage: Producing Musical Theatre.* New York, NY: The Rosen Publishing Group, Inc., 1988.

*Time.* "The Now & Future Queen." December 23, 1966. Retrieved October 19, 2008 (http://www.time.com/time/magazine/article/0,9171,840779,00.html).

Tumbusch, Tom. *Complete Production Guide to Modern Musical Theatre.* New York, NY: Richards Rosen Press, Inc., 1969.

# INDEX

## About the Author

Doretta Lau is an arts and culture writer living in Hong Kong. She acted in a number of high school productions and still enjoys the theater.

## Photo Credits

Cover (background), p. 1 Gaye Gerard/Getty Images; cover (inset), pp. 20–21, 42–43 Shutterstock.com; pp. 4–5 © Robbie Jack/Corbis; pp. 8–9 © Michael Newman/PhotoEdit; p. 11 © www.istockphoto.com/Herbert Bias; pp. 14, 17 © Jim West/The Image Works; p. 24 © James Marshall/Corbis; pp. 26–27 © David Lassman/Syracuse Newspapers/The Image Works; p. 31 © www.istockphoto.com/Joanne Green; pp. 34–35 © Noah Addis/Star Ledger/Corbis; pp. 36–37 © Jeff Greenberg/The Image Works; p. 40 © Chris Barth/Star Ledger/Corbis; pp. 44–45 Lisa Maree Williams/Getty Images; p. 47 © Bob Daemmrich/The Image Works; pp. 48–49 © AP Images; p. 53 © Syracuse Newspapers/Heather Bragman/The Image Works.

Designer: Sam Zavieh; Editor: Bethany Bryan
Photo Researcher: Cindy Reiman